P9-CFT-512

QUIET CORNERS
OF PARIS

✦

Quiet Corners of
PARIS

BY JEAN-CHRISTOPHE NAPIAS

PHOTOGRAPHS BY CHRISTOPHE LEFÉBURE

TRANSLATED BY DAVID DOWNIE

THE LITTLE BOOKROOM ✦ NEW YORK

Book design: Louise Fili Ltd

Printed in China

Library of Congress Cataloging-in-Publication Data

Napias, Jean-Christophe.
[Paris au calme. English]
Quiet corners of Paris : unexpected hideaways, secret courtyards, hidden gardens /
by Jean-Christophe Napias ; photos by Christophe Lefébure ; translated by David Downie.
ISBN 978-1-892145-50-5
p. cm.
Includes index.
ISBN-13: 978-1-892145-50-5 (alk. paper)
ISBN-10: 1-892145-50-2 (alk. paper)
1. Paris (France)—Description and travel. 2. Paris (France)—Buildings, structures, etc.
3. Paris (France)—Pictorial works. I. Lefébure, Christophe. II. Title.
DC707.N2513 2007
914.4'3610484—dc22
2007012322

Published by The Little Bookroom
1755 Broadway, 5th floor
New York NY 10019
editorial@littlebookroom.com
www.littlebookroom.com

Distributed in the U.S. by Random House, in the U.K. and Ireland by Signature Book Services,
and in Europe by Random House International.

2 4 6 8 0 9 7 5 3 1

In memory of William Baranès
For my parents

With thanks to Sandrine, Joseph, Victor, Clair Paulhan,
FB and the great CL

Contents

Foreword

CLOSE YOUR EYES. IT'S THE MIDDLE OF THE AFTERNOON. THE SUN IS SHINING. YOU'RE SITTING ON A LAWN, LEANING YOUR BACK ON AN apple tree. It's a beautiful, mild day filled with the sounds of birds singing, bees buzzing, people chatting. In the distance a church bell rings. You sigh with satisfaction as you re-read a favorite book, totally relaxed. Then suddenly you remember—you're not in the leafy garden of some grand country mansion. You're in Paris. In Paris?

Big cities mean crowds, confusion, hustle, bustle and noise—they're like a giant with chronic indigestion. But beyond the giant's bubbling belly, by some miracle other body parts are spared gastric distress. That's why eructating, chaotic place de la Bastille in eastern Paris, and the quiet, calm, narrow roads of Cité Florale on the city's south side, seem to belong to entirely different worlds.

Paris may well be the most beautiful city on earth, but as any resident or visitor knows, it's not exactly a haven of peace...too much traffic, too much noise, too many people.

Parisians face the rumbling daily reality of the City of Might and seem to feel they have three options: put up with it, cocoon cozily at home, or get out. And that's exactly what Parisians increasingly do—they leave town on weekends or become neo-rural refugees in the seemingly evergreen French countryside.

But for those who choose to stay in Paris—and for visitors, too—all is far from lost! This handy little book's job is to lead questers to the city's magical islands—famous or unknown—where their thirst for silent escapes can be slaked.

Most of the places listed are out of doors and open to the public, with a pleasant green-garden atmosphere. They're beautiful spots—as the book's photographs clearly show. That's not surprising. It's hard to imagine an ugly, hard-edged place being restful.

A word to Parisians worried that we've unveiled "their" secret places. Calm down—no need to get agitated. The madding crowd is a predictable beast, rushing from one trendy, new, hip, must-see spot to the next. When it comes to still backwaters, to uncluttered nooks and noiseless crannies, the crowds simply shy away, uninterested. Crowds draw crowds. Quiet places stay quiet. That's a good thing for those of us who like life on the quiet side.

Cour Carrée du Louvre

COURTYARD, MUSÉE DU LOUVRE

1ST ARRONDISSEMENT

Entrances: rue de Rivoli, cour Napoléon, quai François-Mitterrand, rue de l'Amiral-de-Coligny

Métro: Louvre-Rivoli, Palais-Royal-Musée-du-Louvre

Open daily

✦

IT MAY SEEM UNUSUAL TO START A QUEST FOR QUIET IN THE COURTYARD OF PARIS' MOST POPULAR MUSEUM. MORE THAN SIX MILLION visitors besiege the labyrinthine Louvre every year. The wealth of the museum's collections makes the head spin.

But not the Cour Carrée. The name means "square courtyard" and, yes, each side is the same length—112.5 meters to be precise. That works out to more than 12,500 square meters, not bad for a courtyard. Kings François I and Henri II—and their heirs right up to Louis XIV—built it on the southwest corner of Emperor Philippe Auguste's Louvre, atop medieval foundations.

The best way to enter is through the gateway facing the church of St-Germain-l'Auxerrois in rue de l'Amiral-de-Coligny—the Louvre's original main entrance. As you'd expect, the doors opened toward the city, not the countryside. The facade's spectacular colonnade is 175 meters long and bears the coat-of-arms of Louis XIV. It's grandiose, majestic and imposing—like the courtyard within.

Step through the gateway and the sound of the city is suddenly squelched by the courtyard's thick, history-clad walls. Passing tourists are similarly silenced. Do the walls

somehow possess the power to make those inside them respectful and retiring? In summer's heat, the phenomenon is all the more startling.

Intrepid visitors scrutinize step-by-step the courtyard's countless sculpted marvels—though they might want to consider hiring a guide to help them fully appreciate the site.

Others will be happy to sit on the benches that frame the courtyard's central fountain, or find a secluded spot in one of the niches in the north facade, seemingly designed for leisurely lounging. From noon to 3pm the courtyard draws sun-worshipers and those who like to laze siesta-style, plus a handful of bookish types and picnickers with sandwiches from Chez Julien.

To appreciate just how quiet the Cour Carrée really is, step through the archway toward I. M. Pei's Louvre Pyramid in the cour Napoléon, a study in swarming, mass tourism. Reality check? This is the twenty-first century, after all.

Galerie Véro-Dodat

1ST ARRONDISSEMENT

Entrances: 19, rue Jean-Jacques-Rousseau; 2, rue du Bouloi
Métro: Louvre-Rivoli, Palais-Royal-Musée-du-Louvre
Open Mon-Sat 7am-10pm (closed Sun, holidays)

✦

AMONG OTHER CHALLENGES, PARIS' HISTORIC COVERED GALLERIES ARE THREATENED IN EQUAL MEASURE BY NEGLECT (FOR INSTANCE, THE Passage Ben-Aïad in the second arrondissement) and deadening gentrification (the Passage des Princes, also in the second arrondissement).

Here's one *passage* that's managing to succeed with understated style in the delicate balancing act. Véro and Dodat, enterprising butcher-caterers, built this neoclassical gallery in the first half of the 1800s, to link the wholesale food market at Les Halles and the posh Palais-Royal. And they cashed in on the location, location, location and foot traffic. There are few crowds nowadays, however—just the rare, lost tourist and curio-hunting stroller.

Curiosities abound, especially on the high end of the market, from the stylish Franco Maria Ricci (FMR) bookshop to upscale decorative arts galleries like Galérie du Passage and Eric Philippe. There's a seller of antique books, and Robert Capia's intriguing emporium of vintage dolls and puppets, plus a photo gallery and more. And let's not forget the little old-fashioned restaurant with a menu as modest as it is affordable.

What of the covered gallery's stylish nineteenth-century decorations? Surprisingly, the great neoclassical authority, Italian *professore* Mario Praz, somehow failed to mention the Galérie Véro-Dodat in his seminal collection of walks in Paris.

Nonetheless, there's no lack of attention to lavish detail, from the marble checkerboard paving and molded fronds and roses, to the ceilings painted with mythological figures—Apollo, Minerva, Ceres and Mercury. Kitsch? Absolutely. That doesn't stop visitors from pausing at the end of the gallery's forty-meter length, turning on their heels and strolling it again. Slowly.

Jardin(s) du Palais-Royal

PALAIS-ROYAL GARDEN[S]

1ST ARRONDISSEMENT

Entrances: rue de Montpensier, rue de Beaujolais, rue de Valois, Palais-Royal
Métro: Palais-Royal-Musée-du-Louvre
Open daily 7:30am-8:30pm

✦

SOME PARISIANS CAMPAIGN FOR THE PLURAL SPELLING, BUT EITHER WAY THE PALAIS-ROYAL GARDEN(S) ARE SINGULARLY APPEALING. THE history of this secluded enclave—from the days when it was called "Palais-Cardinal" to the present—would fill volumes. Armand-Jean du Plessis, aka Richelieu, was the cardinal in question, and the spot's roistering heyday of centuries gone by couldn't be more different than the soulful, nostalgia-embued Palais-Royal of today. It's hard to fathom that in the late eighteenth century a kind of circus structure stood where the central fountain now splashes away. Could this really be the same place Balzac described in *Lost Illusions?* "Ladies of the night rushed from all over Paris to 'do the Palais.' The women had a look that doesn't exist anymore—the way they wore their low-cut dresses open halfway down the back and very low in front, too, and their strange, eye-catching hairstyles. By night these ladies drew such crowds to the wooden walkways that people shuffled along at a snail's pace, as if in a procession or at a masked ball. The pace didn't trouble anyone and allowed for examination of the merchandise. It was at once horrible and joyful. The showy flesh of shoulders and throats sparkled amid the near-uniform darkness of the men's clothes, making for marvelous contrasts. Pillars of the establishment stood cheek by jowl with the most sinister types."

Things certainly have changed. Nowadays the park pulls in a largely prim-and-proper clientele, people who walk quietly along the porticoes' 180 arches, peering into the boutiques—unusual, old-fashioned or sumptuous. The best spot? That's purely personal. You can bet, though, that everyone will enjoy resting for a spell on one of the Jean-Michel Wilmotte designer armchairs, maybe somewhere near the courtyard's colonnaded perimeter, in the scattered sun and shade of the linden trees, for instance, or by Frédéric Castaing's one-of-a-kind shop selling valuable signed manuscripts and letters. Once you've settled in, you might even want to try reading one of the page-turning crime novels Castaing pens after hours.

Place Dauphine

1ST ARRONDISSEMENT

Western tip of Île de la Cité

Entrances: rue de Harlay, place du Pont-Neuf

Métro: Pont-Neuf

Open daily

✦

J*E SUIS LE DAUPHIN DE LA PLACE DAUPHINE ET LA PLACE BLANCHE A MAUVAISE MINE*...EVERY TRUE PARISIAN KNOWS THAT HIT FROM YESteryear, *Il est 5 heures Paris s'éveille*, sung by Jacques Dutron (with catchy words by Jacques Lanzmann). Dauphin—meaning heir to the throne—is right: place Dauphine was built by Henri IV in honor of his son and heir, the future Louis XIII. It was Paris' second royal square, after the place des Vosges. The triangular layout reflects the island's topography more than any architect's conscious choice of geometry. The original, early-1600s buildings of brick and stone were three stories tall. At the time, three rows of them enclosed the triangular space. But in 1874, the eastern row of buildings was demolished to ease access to, and to allow views of, what was supposed to be—but never became—the new Palais de Justice's main entrance.

Today the peaceful place is the haunt of *pétanque* players and nostalgic fans of Yves Montand and Simone Signoret, who lived at number 15. Others follow the trail of Georges Simenon, once a regular at the square's cafés. Literary types seek the stomping grounds of André Breton, who used the square as a backdrop for several scenes of uneasy sexual repression in *Nadja*. He and other surrealists saw the curves of the Seine as a supine woman, her triangle of pubic hair represented, naturally, by place Dauphine.

PLACE NUMER THE

Rue Payenne

3RD ARRONDISSEMENT
Métro: Saint-Paul, Chemin-Vert
Musée Cognacq-Jay: 8, rue Elzévir
Open Tue-Sun 10am-5:40pm (closed Mon, holidays)
Centre Culturel Suédois (Swedish Cultural Center): 11, rue Payenne
Expositions open Tue-Sun noon-6pm (closed Mon)
Square Georges-Cain: 8, rue Payenne
Open Mon-Fri 7:30am-5:30pm (winter); 7:30am-9:30pm (summer); weekends 9am

✦

RUE PAYENNE IS A THREE-IN-ONE OF ARCHITECTURAL AND GARDEN TRANQUILITY IN A CORNER OF THE MARAIS OVERRUN ON WEEKENDS by herds of shoppers and culture seekers. No boutiques or bustle on this stretch, though. The 342 meters of sidewalk offer several surprises. Start with the Cognacq-Jay Museum; there's no admission charge here or in any of Paris' municipal museums. The entrance is on rue Elzévir. The museum's eighteenth-century collections were put together by Ernest Cognacq and his wife, Louise Jay, founders of the Samaritaine department store. Furnishings, decorative objects, sculptures and paintings fill twenty thematic rooms on three floors. The setting is the handsome Hôtel de Donon, a sixteenth-century townhouse. Rarely crowded, it emanates the intimate

charm typical of small house-museums and also boasts a pocket-sized French formal garden on the rue Payenne. The museum may seem deserted, but the garden is downright empty—hardly anyone steps into it.

Back to the rue Payenne and a slice of Scandinavia at the Swedish Cultural Center. Here it's the other way around: the entrance is on rue Payenne, the garden's out back on rue Elzévir. This delicious nook even has a lawn you can sit on—you *should* sit on—to take full advantage in fine weather of the center's outdoor café and courtyard. Likewise, you're encouraged to visit the exhibitions and check out events in the Hôtel de Marle, the center's home since 1971.

And for the kicker, how about hitting the square Georges-Cain on rue Payenne across from the Swedish Cultural Center? Cain was the first

head-curator of the nearby Carnavalet Museum, which explains the garden's unusual architectural fragments. They come from the Carnavalet's reserves, but were originally part of the ruined Tuileries Palace, or at Saint-Germain-en-Laye and Saint-Cloud. The stonework blends in nicely with the garden's other elements, including the orangerie of the Hôtel Le-Peletier-de-Saint-Fargeau edging the property; an impressive fig tree; and a Maillol sculpture, *L'Île-de-France*. Maillol's enigmatic, curvaceous bronze girl-child in her birthday suit seems to draw curious glances whatever the season.

Jardin Saint-Gilles-Grand-Veneur

SAINT-GILLES-GRAND-VENEUR GARDEN

3RD ARRONDISSEMENT

Entrances: rue des Arquebusiers, rue Villehardouin

Métro: Chemin-Vert

Open daily 9am-5pm (winter); 9am-9pm (summer)

✦

IF WE HAD TO COME UP WITH A SHORTLIST OF FAVORITES IN THIS BOOK, THE SAINT-GILLES-GRAND-VENEUR GARDEN WOULD EASILY BE IN THE top three. The spot has everything going for it. First, it was smart enough to hide itself away from the street between a group of buildings. They seem pretty unprepossessing but are compensated for by the gorgeous facade of the Hôtel du Grand-Veneur. You're miles from the noisy city, barely audible and quickly forgotten. Every half hour the atmospheric silence is pricked gently by the tolling bell of nearby Saint-Denys-du-Saint-Sacrement—a nice provincial touch. The garden is a felicitous marriage of maple trees and climbing, trellised roses. Look carefully and you'll find the Catherine Deneuve stretching its lithe branches. The four small lawns lend a further bucolic touch. Among the thousand-and-one things Parisians usually do in the city's open spaces—wolfing sandwiches, reading newspapers, fiddling with iPods, burning up cell-phone credit, making a date (multiple dates, where applicable), snapping great pics, jawing with pals, breaking up, killing time, watching kids play, walking the dog, sunbathing, worrying about interest rates—the best pastime of all is also the simplest: doing nothing at all.

Hôtels du Marais

TOWNHOUSES OF THE MARAIS

3RD ARRONDISSEMENT
Métro: Saint-Paul, Hôtel-de-Ville
Musée Carnavalet: 23, rue de Sévigné
Open Tue-Sat 10am-6pm (closed Mon, holidays)
Hôtel de Soubise: 60, rue des Francs-Bourgeois
Open Wed-Mon 1:45-5:45pm (closed Tue)

✦

ONE OF THE CHARMS OF CENTRAL PARIS IS ITS WEALTH OF HISTORIC MONUMENTS. THE MARAIS NEIGHBORHOOD HAS MORE THAN ITS share. But to find and take advantage of the Marais' quiet corners, you've got to be lucky, wily or downright dogged. Small and sometimes jammed, the cour de la Victoire inside the Carnavalet museum is seductively appealing. Much of the magic derives from the boxwood hedges—trimmed *à la française*—and the timelessness of the townhouse where seventeenth-century epistolary queen Madame de Sévigné lived and loved. A quieter, more spacious spot is only minutes west: the courtyard of the Hôtel de Soubise. Tables and chairs await visitors under the colonnaded portico that graces three of the court's sides. In normal times you'd be able to enjoy other Marais-mansion courtyards—at the Archives nationales and the vast, unsung Hôtel de Rohan, for instance—but, sadly, anti-terror regulations don't allow it.

Galerie Karsten Greve

3RD ARRONDISSEMENT
5, rue Debelleyme
Métro: Saint-Sébastien-Froissart
Open Tue-Sat 11am-7pm (closed Sun, Mon)

✦

EXCEPT ON OPENING NIGHTS, THERE'S HARDLY ANYONE (NO ONE AT ALL, SOME CLAIM) IN PARIS' CONTEMPORARY ART GALLERIES. SO BE it. This isn't the place to tackle issues of old vs. new. Judge for yourself what "empty" means.

The third arrondissement has plenty of prestigious art showcases, Karsten Greve's Paris operation among them (he runs three galleries in Europe all told). It opened in 1989 in a handsome townhouse. Step through the monumental carriage gateway into the cobbled court and you know you're at the high end—not the rough edge—of the contemporary scene. Most of the photographers Greve represents do vintage- or nineteenth-century-style work. The gallery's two wings show large-format photos—Thomas Brummett's plant pics (printed with an Iris printer), for instance, and Lynn Davis' or Sally Mann's extra-large landscapes.

A visit here is always win-win: beautiful setting, free entrance, top-quality art and, last but not least, utter peace. What more can you ask for?

Cloître des Billettes

BILLETTES CLOISTER

4TH ARRONDISSEMENT
24, rue des Archives
Métro: Hôtel-de-Ville
Open daily 10am-7pm

✦

"HERE, THEN, IS THAT LITTLE CLOISTER THAT SHARES WITH US ITS SILENCE, A SILENCE OF THE FIFTEENTH CENTURY, AND ITS PENsive arcades that faithfully convey the image of a questing soul who searches within as we are no longer capable of searching."

That's how writer Julien Green evokes Les Billettes—the only remaining medieval cloister in town—in his 1980 book, *Paris*. Let's keep reading: "It was late afternoon and within those walls, in the shadow of the thickset columns, was a token of the treasure that is daily torn from us and whose utter loss would kill off in us what goodness remains: silence. It was not disturbed but rather deepened by the clear, regular dripping of water into a small basin..."

Nowadays the streetside atmosphere on rue des Archives—clogged with noisy cars and stuffed with gay bars, restaurants and boutiques—doesn't exactly stimulate inner scrutiny.

Still, by some minor miracle silence survives within the cloister, measured believe it or not by the perennial drip and plash of that same leaking faucet and an overfilled watering can. A challenge, perhaps, to time passing...

Clos des Blancs-Manteaux

BLANCS-MANTEAUX ENCLOSED GARDEN

4TH ARRONDISSEMENT
21, rue des Blancs-Manteaux
Métro: Hôtel-de-Ville, Rambuteau
Open weekends (closed weekdays)

✦

AT 21 RUE DES BLANCS-MANTEAUX, THERE'S A CO-OP DAYCARE CENTER, A MUNICIPAL PRESCHOOL AND A CHILDREN'S NURSERY-GARDEN used by thousands of kids each year. In other words, the kind of place to flee if you're looking for tranquility...a place to flee on weekdays, that is. Because the kiddies aren't around on weekends. That's when you can enjoy the spot in splendid isolation. Recently created and little known, the park is dedicated to the memory of Princess Diana. It's well ensconced among surrounding buildings.

Quietly you can tiptoe through tulips—and hundreds of other species of flowers, fruits, vegetables and aromatic herbs. Meditative types will want to linger in the leafy forecourt, on a bench, amid trees.

Bibliothèque Forney, Hôtel de Sens

FORNEY LIBRARY, HÔTEL DE SENS

4TH ARRONDISSEMENT
Entrance: 1, rue du Figuier
Métro: Pont-Marie, Saint-Paul
Open Tue-Sat 1:30-7pm (closed Sun, Mon)

✦

LIBRARIES FALL INTO THAT SELECT GROUP OF PLACES WHERE THE PUBLIC IS INVITED TO BE QUIET AND RESPECTFUL OR RISK PUNISHMENT by raised eyebrow and reprimand. In other words, they're naturally tranquil. The Forney library specializes in the decorative and fine arts. Its appeal is manyfold. A municipal property, it's open to all, rarely thronged, and housed in a medieval mansion with exceptional architectural features inside and out. There is a fine French garden in the rear.

Jardin de l'hôtel de Sully

HÔTEL DE SULLY GARDEN

4TH ARRONDISSEMENT

Entrances: 62, rue Saint-Antoine; 7, place des Vosges

Métro: Saint-Paul

Open daily 9am-6pm

✦

NEIGHBORHOOD RESIDENTS THINK OF THE HÔTEL DE SULLY'S HIDDEN GARDEN AS A RARE URBAN WRINKLE, A SHORTCUT BETWEEN noisy rue Saint-Antoine and sublime place des Vosges. It only takes a minute to traverse, but the setting is splendid: a pocket-sized French garden tucked between a sumptuous Louis XIII mansion and its *orangerie*—what habitués call *le petit Sully*.

The four tiny lawns edged by clipped boxwood hedges are off limits—the gardener's preserve—but the four stone benches set around them welcome visitors' posteriors. That means seating is scarce and sought after, especially between noon and 2pm. The lucky few avoid the envious glaces of latecomers who have little choice but to take their newspapers and brown bags elsewhere. Speaking of which, a good place to buy a sandwich is Pasta Linea, at 9, rue de Turenne. Their round loaves filled with luscious antipasti and peppery arugula justify the five-minute walk. History buffs might want to sit in the Sully's garden and plunge into Charles Sorel's *Histoire comique de Francion* (Gallimard, 1996). It paints an enlightening picture of French mores during the early reign of Louis XIII—the neighborhood's seventeenth-century heyday. If music's your thing, try *L'Orchestre de Louis XIII* (Alia Vox), compiled by Jordi Savall.

Village Saint-Paul

4TH ARRONDISSEMENT

Entrances: rue Saint-Paul, rue Charlemagne, rue des Jardins-Saint-Paul

Métro: Saint-Paul, Sully-Morland

Open daily

✦

SOME URBAN REHAB PROJECTS WIND UP KILLING THE SPIRIT OF PLACE THEY WERE INTENDED TO REVIVE. THERE'S NO QUESTION THAT THE Saint Paul "village" suffered this fate to a degree, though less so than many other 1960s-'70s remakes. How often was the wrecking ball preferred instead?

Hardly anyone comes here. A pity, because some of the shops inside the labyrinthine compound are noteworthy. For instance, the Sylvain Calvier vintage photography gallery, stuffed from floor to rafters with images from all periods and places.

The best time to explore the village is at dusk, when the streetlamps are lit. Inviting atmosphere guaranteed!

That dusky appeal spreads to surrounding streets and alleys such as passage Saint-Paul, rue Éginhard and rue des Jardins-Saint-Paul (offering views from its western side of Emperor Philippe Auguste's twelfth-century city walls). The ghosts of medieval Paris seem to haunt these empty alleys, which are as lovely as they are disquieting.

Centre culturel irlandais

IRISH CULTURAL CENTER

5TH ARRONDISSEMENT

Entrance: Collège des Irlandais, 5, rue des Irlandais

Métro: Place-Monge, RER: Luxembourg

Exhibitions open Tue-Sat 2-6pm (Wed 8pm) and Sun 12:30-2:30pm

✦

CULTIVATED ESCAPISTS KNOW THE DRILL WITH PARIS' MANY FOREIGN CULTURAL CENTERS. SOME OCCUPY SUMPTUOUS SEVENTH arrondissement mansions (the Italian and Latin American). Others settle for modest embassy annexes. The Irish center animates a townhouse used by the Irish Catholic collegiate community since 1775. In the 1700s the road was called rue du Cheval-Vert. (It got its Irish moniker under Napoléon.) The center re-opened in 2002 after restorations to the diminutive chapel of St. Patrick. The courtyard and its chestnut trees came through unmolested. Wonderfully unknown, it is the ideal place to read in peace and quiet. Why not open a book by Ireland's great James Patrick Donleavy? His work is imbued with a unique stylistic touch that merges truculence and poetry. *The Ginger Man* caused a scandal in its day, for its earthy, freewheeling rawness. Some readers prefer *The Beastly Beatitudes of Balthazar B*, which opens: "He was born in Paris in a big white house on a small square off Avenue Foch." Later, life gets kind of complicated for him. Speaking of the "Irish touch," if you fancy a pint wander over to the Hideout (11 rue Pot-de-Fer), a little pub steeped in Irishness, with elbow-lifting Happy Hour prices. Not exactly the same atmosphere…but variety is the secret of pleasure, isn't it?

Jardin de l'École normale supérieure

ÉCOLE NORMALE SUPÉRIEURE GARDEN

5TH ARRONDISSEMENT

Entrance: 45, rue d'Ulm

Métro: Censier-Daubenton, Place-Monge, RER: Luxembourg

Open weekday school hours (when in session)

✦

WHAT UNITES LOUIS PASTEUR, JEAN JAURÈS, HENRI BERGSON, LÉON BLUM, CHARLES PÉGUY, VLADIMIR JANKÉLÉVITCH, JEAN-Paul Sartre, Raymond Aron, Paul Nizan, Léopold Sédar Senghor, Julien Gracq, Georges Pompidou, Jacqueline de Romilly, Jean-François Revel, Dominique Fernandez, Michel Serres, Pierre Bourdieu, Pierre-Gilles de Gennes, Jacques Derrida, Régis Debray, Alain Juppé, Guy Hocquenghem, Laurent Fabius, Bernard-Henri Lévy, André Comte-Sponville, Marie Darrieussecq and Alexandre Adler? Simple. They all attended this prestigious school. Did they, perhaps, wander down this self-same garden path and sit at this very table? Don't be cowed. Relax and enjoy the leafy green garden of this venerable institution of higher learning.

Hôtel des Grandes Écoles

5TH ARRONDISSEMENT
Entrance: 75, rue du Cardinal-Lemoine
Métro: Cardinal-Lemoine, Place-Monge
Open daily

✦

DID THE INVENTOR OF THE "CHARM HOTEL" CONCEPT REALIZE HOW SUCCESSFUL—AD NAUSEUM—THE LABEL WOULD BECOME? HAPPILY, the appellation rings true at this address. Breach the carriage door and discover a magnificent freestanding house opening onto a flower-filled, tree-studded garden. The owners should be applauded for avoiding the loud luxe look, preferring instead a family feel. The hotel's rooms are nicely furnished and modestly priced. Peace reigns. There are no TVs. Enjoy this rare refuge in fine weather when you can breakfast or take tea in the garden. The experience transports you straight out of the city, though the clientele is as cosmopolitan as they come. And don't even dream of a last-minute reservation: rooms are booked solid far, far ahead.

Grande Mosquée de Paris

GRAND MOSQUE OF PARIS

5TH ARRONDISSEMENT

Entrance: 2, place du Puits-de-l'Ermite

Métro: Place-Monge, Censier-Daubenton

Open Sat-Thur 9am-noon and 2-6pm (closed Fridays and Muslim holidays)

✦

LOWER THAN THE LOWEST LOW-COST AIRFARE! FOR A MERE THREE EUROS YOU CAN TRAVEL FROM PARIS TO THE ORIENT BY WALKING over to the Grande Mosquée. This Hispano-Moorish sacred site of Islam was built in the 1920s in homage to the 100,000 Muslims who fought and died for France in the First World War. Non-Muslims can take private discovery tours of the gardens and building, which were inspired by the Mosque of Fez. Overrun by tourists, not to mention the faithful who flock here on Fridays (that's why it's closed to visitors on Fridays), this is a popular spot. So, to take full advantage of the courtyards, patios and gardens and get a foretaste of Paradise (one of the compound's themes), there's a simple solution: visit on a sunny Sunday morning. Escapism guaranteed!

Arènes de Lutèce

ARENA OF LUTÈCE

5TH ARRONDISSEMENT
Entrances: rue des Arènes, rue de Navarre, rue Monge
Métro: Place-Monge, Jussieu, Cardinal-Lemoine
Open daily 8am-5:30pm (winter); 9am-9:30pm (summer)

✦

THIS MAGICAL SPOT MARKS THE SITE OF PARIS' LARGEST GALLO-ROMAN RUIN, BUILT IN THE THIRD CENTURY A.D. THE ARENA WAS LONG among Gaul's biggest, with seating for 15,000 spectators—a combination bread-and-circuses-cum-theater venue. The stage is still visible.

Nowadays instead of lions, people kick or pitch balls around: this is the headquarters of the Arènes de Lutèce gravel-bowling club, after all. Speaking of which, one of the neighborhood's most illustrious residents was *pétanque*-loving essayist and publisher Jean Paulhan, the éminence grise of French literature, who lived in a handsome English-style house with a garden on rue des Arènes. He organized regular *pétanque* matches here with Parisian luminaries merrily joining in. They included Marcel Jouhandeau (who was a lousy bowler, reportedly), Jacques Audiberti, Claude Simon (who settled on place Monge nearby to be able to painlessly participate in weekend morning matches), Maurice Toesca, Yves Berg, Jérôme Lindon, Raymond Queneau.

Contemporary publisher Claire Paulhan still remembers watching with her famous grandfather from a window of his house as the harmless heifer-corridas—sans death blow finale—played themselves out below in the Arènes in the 1950s-'60s.

PELOUSE
AU REPOS

Jardin Alpin, Jardin des Plantes

ALPINE GARDEN, BOTANICAL GARDEN

5TH ARRONDISSEMENT

Entrances: place Valhubert, rue Buffon, rue Cuvier,
rue Geoffroy-Saint-Hilaire, rue Linné
Métro: Gare-d'Austerlitz, Jussieu, Place-Monge
Open daily 8am-5:30pm

✦

SOMEWHERE WITHIN THE TWENTY-THREE AMPLE HECTARES OF THE JARDIN DES PLANTES YOU'LL ALWAYS FIND A PEACEFUL NOOK. YOU can choose, for instance, among the greenhouses, the labyrinth or...the astonishing alpine garden. Created in 1931, it harbors over 2,000 alpine species, grouped by geographical origin. The rockeries offer a veritable round-the-globe trot from Corsica to the Alps, Pyrénées, Cévennes, Caucasses, Himalayas, Japan, China, the Balkans and North America. Insiders know that the Asiatic pistachio tree that grows here allowed botanist Sébastien Vaillant to establish his early-1700s theory of plant gender and sexuality.

Casual strollers enjoying the leafy lanes might not appreciate just how difficult it is to reproduce the original environmental conditions needed by each of these plants from far-flung climes. But everyone can grasp the amusing paradox of alpine plants thriving in a sunken garden three meters below the surrounding street level.

Musée Eugène-Delacroix

6TH ARRONDISSEMENT
Entrance: 6, rue de Furstenberg
Métro: Mabillon, Saint-Germain-des-Prés
Open Wed-Mon 9:30am-5pm (closed Tue; and some holidays)

✦

ONE OF THE GROUND RULES FOR INCLUSION IN THIS BOOK IS FREE ACCESS—MEANING NO ENTRANCE FEE. BUT THIS EXCEPTIONAL SITE justifies an exception to the rule: we encourage you to pony up the five euros that will get you into this national museum. It's well worth it. Parsimonious visitors can wait until the first Sunday of each month, or July 14th: entrance is gratis!

"The view of my little garden and the uplifting character of my painting studio always fill me with pleasure," Delacroix liked to say. Visitors today feel similar emotions in this miraculous harbor of peace in the heart of Saint-Germain-des-Prés.

Musée Zadkine

6TH ARRONDISSEMENT

Entrance: 100 bis, rue d'Assas

Métro: Notre-Dame-des-Champs, Vavin, RER: Port-Royal

Open Tue-Sun 10am-6pm (closed Mon)

✦

THIS LITTLE MUSEUM COMES JUST THE WAY WE LIKE THEM: AT A REMOVE FROM ROADS AND BUSTLING SIDEWALKS. HAPPINESS HERE takes the form of a garden, a house, a sculptor's studio and artworks nestled in the greenery.

Welcome to Ossip Zadkine's place. He lived and worked on the premises from 1928 until his death in 1967. Russian by birth, Zadkine arrived in Paris in 1909 and—according to the *Petit Larousse* dictionary—engaged in "a variety of Cubism at times displaying baroque and decorative tendencies, at others expressionist tendencies."

The Zadkine Museum opened in 1982, and thanks to donations by his widow Valentine Prax, includes some 300 sculptures. They fill four rooms, each covering a distinct period in the artist's career. The garden-studio hosts temporary exhibitions.

Cour du Mûrier, École nationale des beaux-arts

MÛRIER COURTYARD, ÉCOLE NATIONALE DES BEAUX-ARTS

6TH ARRONDISSEMENT

Entrance: 14, rue Bonaparte

Métro: Saint-Germain-des-Prés

Open weekdays 8am-8pm (when school is in session)

✦

AS YOU VISIT PARIS' FINE ARTS ACADEMY YOU MIGHT RUN INTO PROFESSORS WHO ARE BIG NAMES IN CONTEMPORARY ART: CHRISTIAN Boltanski, Claude Closky, Fabrice Hybert or Annette Messager. Some sensitive visitors even claim to feel the presence of other illustrious souls trained here—Eugène Delacroix, Théodore Géricault, Antoine Bourdelle, Edgar Degas, Roland Topor or Olivier Debré. And what of tomorrow's budding talents?

Whatever. Take a tool around the delightful cour du Mûrier, which is set in the former cloister of the Petits-Augustins church, recast in the 1800s by architect Félix Duban. He turned it into a classical-period atrium surrounded by arcades and graced with a central fountain. The Pompeii-style paintings and plaster casts of the Parthenon's friezes were added later. The courtyard's decor is the only example of its kind in Paris, and is all the more enjoyable because of the setting's remarkable tranquility.

SALON de THÉ
L'heure Gourmande
RESTAURATION CHOISIE

Passage Dauphine

6TH ARRONDISSEMENT

Entrances: 30, rue Dauphine; 27, rue Mazarine

Métro: Odéon, Mabillon

Open daily

✦

BREATHE IN, BREATHE OUT. THERE AREN'T MANY OF THESE LITTLE PASSAGEWAYS LEFT IN PARIS, PLACES WHERE YOU CAN SLIP BETWEEN the buildings and escape from the madding crowd, the cars, the noise—the city, in short. Paris seems to breathe freely in this calm, cool oasis, where fig and olive trees grow, and a tea salon spreads its tables, suggesting a pleasant way to make the rite of passage through the Passage Dauphine last a little longer.

Cour de Rohan

6TH ARRONDISSEMENT

Entrances: rue du Jardinet; 2, cour du Commerce-Saint-André

Métro: Odéon

Open daily (often closed weekends)

✦

THE STRING OF SMALL COURTYARDS THAT COMPOSE THE VENERABLE COUR DE ROHAN IS POSSESSED OF MAGIC AND IMBUED WITH A FANCY-free, provincial feel. Visit while you can—the lucky few who live here will eventually get permission to close access to the courtyards with a digital lock on the gate, the kind of locks that are gradually shutting off this theatrical city's wings to intrepid pedestrian-explorers.

The cour de Rohan not only satisfies your thirst for quietude. It offers other attractions. One is the antique *pas-de-mule*, a three-footed metal stool that ladies and robed priests—and the seniors of old—used for a leg-up into their carriage. It might just be the only *pas-de-mule* left in Paris. There's also a well—one of the city's 365 known wells—with a pully and gargoyle-sculpted rim from the fourteenth century. Last but not least, in the courtyard closest to the cour Commerce-Saint-André, you can see the base of a tower from the medieval city walls of Emperor Philippe Auguste.

Jardin du Luxembourg

LUXEMBOURG GARDENS

6TH ARRONDISSEMENT

Entrances: rue Guynemer, rue de Vaugirard, rue de Médicis, rue Auguste-Comte, boulevard Saint-Michel

Métro: Odéon, RER: Luxembourg

Open daily (hours vary widely according to the season; 7:30am or 8:15am-4:15pm or 9:15pm)

✦

PARIS GARDENS ARE LIKE THE CITY'S DENIZENS: ON A BAD DAY OR AT THE WRONG TIME THEY'RE BAD NEWS. THE LUXEMBOURG IS THE perfect example of this. It's not an easy customer, so to speak. Surrounded by arteries often thrumming with traffic (boulevard Saint-Michel, rue de Vaugirard), and itself thronged at certain times of day, it seems to throw down the gauntlet to questers of quiet isolation. So you have to do the rounds, circle the park carefully and seek out that rare, quiet corner where suddenly the pressing flesh and city disappear. Find that miraculously empty chair, sit down, close your eyes and breathe at last. And maybe think back to Hemingway, penniless in his early Paris years, and how he hunted pigeons in these gorgeous gardens.

Jardin botanique de la faculté de pharmacie

BOTANICAL GARDEN, FACULTY OF PHARMACOLOGY

6TH ARRONDISSEMENT
Entrance: 4, avenue de l'Observatoire
Métro: RER Port-Royal
Open weekdays 9am-7pm

✦

NOW HERE'S A WORTHWHILE SPOT. THERE'S NO SIGNAGE, SO TO GET IN, GO TO THE END AND TURN LEFT. IT'S AS EASY AS THAT. ONCE there, you'll discover a botanical garden devised for students of the faculty of pharmacology of Paris University. Obviously the brilliance and abundance of the garden's color and light, the strength of the scents and the volume of the insects buzzing around, depend entirely on the season and the hour of the day. You get it: the *jardin botanique* isn't at its best in winter. But in any season, this little groomed plot offers the secluded tranquility of its hothouses and plants tagged with Latin binomials. Future pharmacists really do still come here to study the properties of plants commonly used even in modern medicine.

Jardin Catherine-Labouré

CATHERINE-LABOURÉ GARDEN

7TH ARRONDISSEMENT

Entrance: 33, rue de Babylone

Métro: Sèvres-Babylone, Vaneau

Open weekdays 8am-5pm (9am weekends; until 9:30pm in summer)

✦

MAKE SURE YOU'RE ON THE RIGHT SIDEWALK, BECAUSE AT THIS POINT RUE DE BABYLONE IS FLANKED BY TWO PARKS. ON THE even-numbered side is one of Paris' biggest private enclaves, dotted with magnificent old trees. The entrance (for restricted audiences) is 57, rue de Varenne and as any Parisian knows, it leads to the Hôtel de Matignon, aka the Prime Minister's compound.

So unless you have high-powered friends, take the other sidewalk and step into the Jardin Catherine-Labouré instead. No worries. Its charms are abundant. This country-like corner offers 7,000 square meters of grapevines, ornamental berry bushes, and hazelnut, apple and cherry trees. It's crossed by pathways that evoke a crucifix, possibly not entirely by chance, since until 1970 the land belonged to the Filles de la Charité order whose convent lies on the park's left-hand side. Does the piety next door augment the quota of serenity? Perhaps. In any case, a quietude ever rarer in Paris reigns here.

Deyrolle / Le Prince Jardinier

7TH ARRONDISSEMENT
Entrance: 46, rue du Bac
Métro: Rue-du-Bac
Open Mon-Sat 10am-7pm (closed Sun and 1-2pm Mon)

✦

IT'S ALWAYS A PLEASURE TO VISIT THIS VENERABLE GRANDE DAME OF A SHOP NOW NEARLY 175 YEARS OLD. SINCE DEYROLLE OPENED IN RUE du Bac in 1888, it's drawn curio-seekers and collectors from around the world. They mix quietly in this one-of-a-kind Paris taxidermist's workshop-boutique, long known for its stuffed animals, and its magnificent collections of butterflies and other insects, as well as minerals and fossils—and the engraved poster-plates that won the establishment and its original owner renown. Jean-Baptise Deyrolle, a natural-history buff, founded the company in 1831. He discovered a calling as a teacher, and his engraved

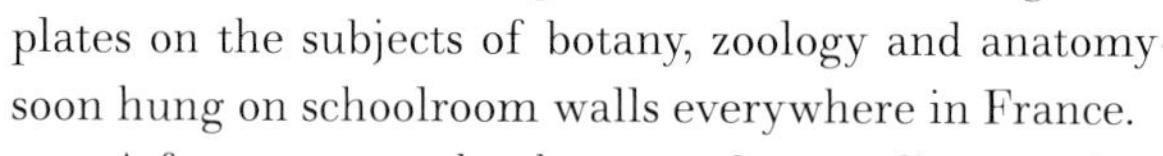

plates on the subjects of botany, zoology and anatomy soon hung on schoolroom walls everywhere in France.

A few years ago the shop was about to disappear but was saved by Louis Albert de Broglie, who now displays his Prince Jardinier product line (a collection of artisanal fragrances, hand-made garden tools and clothing) among the historic collections and curiosities that make this place so special. Deyrolle has been dusted down and dressed up but hasn't lost its magic—it's a den where lions, tigers and elephants roam the jungles of eternity.

Square Récamier

7TH ARRONDISSEMENT
Entrance: 7, rue Récamier
Métro: Sèvres-Babylone
Open weekdays 8am (9am weekends)-5pm (9:30pm in summer)

✦

PARIS IS CHOCK-A-BLOCK WITH GARDENS, PARKS, SQUARES, *CLOS* (ENCLOSED GARDENS), PROMENADES AND SO FORTH, BUT NO ONE seems to know why one garden is called *jardin* and another *parc*. Here we're clearly talking about a *square*—meaning, in French, an enclosed mini-park. It stands at the end of a short street that looks like a cul-de-sac, a kind of decompression chamber between park and city.

Try this experiment: on a Saturday afternoon when rue de Sèvres is a feeding frenzy of commercialism, retreat down rue Récamier (from the corner of boulevard Raspail). Sudden change? You bet. Once out of the inexorable tide flowing toward the Bon Marché department store, here you're in a peaceful pedestrian-only street without a single storefront. Proceed leisurely to the end.

Nestled between buildings that protect it from the bustle, square Récamier isn't just a study in quietude. It's also Mannerist in style. Not very big—no more than 1,500 square meters—nonetheless it's a skillful composition of hillocks, terraces and garden plots, with a wild profusion of plant life. Beyond the big fig tree at the entrance grow magnolias, honeysuckle, rhododendrons and heather. A small waterfall provides the finishing touch to a very pretty picture.

Square Denys-Bühler

7TH ARRONDISSEMENT
Entrance: 147, rue de Grenelle
Métro: Latour-Maubourg
Open weekdays 8am (9am weekends)-5pm (9:30pm in summer)

✦

"THEY'VE ASSASSINATED SILENCE!" LAMENTED FRANÇOIS MAURIAC. "THERE'S NO SILENCE ANYWHERE ANYMORE!" STARTLINGLY, THREE of four French citizens complain of noise-related problems at home, work or elsewhere—pretty much everywhere. Regular overexposure to noise leads to insomnia, limits concentration and reduces attention spans, and can cause high blood pressure and cardiovascular complications—not to mention psychological problems (fatigue, nervousness, moodiness, aggressiveness). We recommend that our most fragile readers spend time here, preferably on a Sunday afternoon. Little known, this garden belonging to the Saint-Jean parish of the French Evangelical Lutheran Church is a delightful, peaceful place that anyone could love as their own back yard. No harm dreaming. And while we're at it, the little half-timbered gatehouse wouldn't be a bad place to nest, either.

Cour d'honneur des Invalides

COURTYARD OF HONOR, LES INVALIDES

7TH ARRONDISSEMENT

Entrance: north entrance of musée de l'Armée on place des Invalides
Métro: Latour-Maubourg, Varenne
Open daily 7:30am-7pm

✦

TRUE, YOU WOULDN'T WANT TO SPEND A WHOLE DAY HERE, BUT THE SITE IS CERTAINLY ASTONISHING ENOUGH FOR A STOPOVER. THE courtyard's size alone is impressive: 102 by 63 meters—about 6,500 square meters all told. That's about half the size of the Louvre's immense Cour Carrée. Now climb to the upstairs portico, where nary a tourist treads. Facing the arcades is a singular sight: canons upended against the walls. Some specimens are spectacular. Wall-mounted plaques pay tribute to fallen soldiers: "In memory of the Spahis who died for France," reads one. "The Union of Zouaves to their comrades who died for France," reads another.

The galerie du Midi houses an imposing statue of Napoléon that once stood atop the Vendôme column. While contemplating the view of the vast courtyard below, does Napoléon's effigy dream of the even higher summits the great man reached? *Sic transit gloria mundi...*

1963
2 INFIRMIERES
ES SOCIALES·I.P.S.A.
CES AMBULANCIERES
URGENCE·SECOURISTES
U SERVICE DE LA
OUGE FRANÇAISE

Cité Odiot

8TH ARRONDISSEMENT

Entrance: 26, rue Washington

Métro: George V

Open

✦

WITH A MERE 10,000 RESIDENTS PER SQUARE KILOMETER, THE EIGHTH ARRONDISSEMENT TIES WITH THE FIRST ARRONDISSEment for Paris' lowest population density. However, it's probably number one in the arrondissement hit parade when it comes to the density of office buildings. That's why some of the neighborhood's arteries that are so busy on weekdays are deserted at night and on weekends.

But population shifts only marginally affect cité Odiot in rue Washington. Here a certain Jean-Baptiste Odiot, a goldsmith, built his Paris townhouse back in the 1820s. Hardly anything is left of the mansion, which was largely demolished to make way in the 1840s for the buildings you see today. Elegant in its own way, the cité Odiot complex gives on a kind of park, shaded by big trees, carpeted with lawns and dotted with shrubbery and flower beds. The Champs-Elysées seems a million miles away.

Parc Monceau

8TH ARRONDISSEMENT

Entrances: boulevard de Courcelles, avenue Vélasquez,
avenue Ruysdaël, avenue Van-Dyck, rue Rembrandt
Métro: Monceau, Villiers, Courcelles
Open daily 7am-8pm (10pm in summer)

✦

ROMANTIC, HARMONIOUS, PROUSTIAN, MYSTERIOUS, CHIC, LITERARY, MELANCHOLY...THERE'S NO LACK OF ADJECTIVES TO DESCRIBE THE parc Monceau. But is it in fact *quiet* or *calm*? Here's the conclusion of a study by the serious-minded publication BAC, the Bulletin des Amateurs de Calme, dated September 2004: "Upon the insistence of certain members, the board of directors therefore met one Sunday afternoon at the gates of the parc Monceau to begin a new review of said park. They were equipped with a camera and a phonometer. We walked up and down each garden path, crossed legally accessible lawns, rounded the lily pond, and took testimony from the statues of Gounod, Musset, Chopin and Maupassant. While in effect there are many corners in which it is possible to enjoy this handsome park in solitude, it is impossible for us to certify it as 'quiet': nowhere did the phonometer drop below fifty-five decibels; it peaked in places at sixty-five decibels. Therefore, the Bureau unanimously but not without regret once again must refuse to include the parc Monceau in our list of the quietest places in Paris."

And so it was written. Still the judgment seems harsh. The lanes of the parc Monceau hold many a surprise in store for those who know when to stroll down them. That's when the full force of quietude embraces this, one of Paris' most beautiful parks.

Square d'Orléans

9TH ARRONDISSEMENT
Entrance: 80, rue Taitbout
Métro: Trinité, Saint-Georges
Open weekdays

✦

TOOLING AROUND PARIS IS SOMETHING YOU HAVE TO LEARN TO DO RIGHT. THE BEST WAY IS ON FOOT, ALONE OR BY TWOS, WITH AN indispensable accessory: a city map. It's equally advisable to take along a small notebook, so you can record addresses and impressions, plus a camera to refresh your memory. Your eye, instinct and curiosity will do the rest.

Here, for instance, you've got to know that by stepping through the threshold of 80, rue Taitbout, you'll discover one of the arrondissement's quietest spots. In the first half of the 1800s, an English architect designed this compound with three courtyards. The British touch is particularly evident in the central courtyard, with its fountain and surrounding basement level.

Back in the heyday of the Nouvelle-Athènes architectural style, this address was particularly sought-after by artists. Residents included painters (Édouard Dubufe), writers (Alexandre Dumas), the celebrated dancer Taglioni, the sculptor Dantan and the pianist Zimmermann (among whose students were Gounod and Bizet). But the square's most famous inhabitant was doubtless Frédéric Chopin, who lived at number 9 during his love affair with George Sand. She had her own apartment here at number 5, and she kept it until 1849. When Sand moved out, the next renter was none other than…Charles Baudelaire.

Cité de Trévise

9TH ARRONDISSEMENT

Entrances: rue Richer, rue Bleue

Métro: Cadet, Bonne-Nouvelle, Poissonnière

Open

✦

"THIS COURTYARD COMPLEX OFFERS THE MOST AGREEABLE OF ALL RETREATS FROM THE CACOPHONY OF BUSINESS AND PLEASURE." SO wrote the real estate promoter when he advertised the building back in the mid-1800s. While business and pleasure are no longer what they were, this courtyard complex continues to offer residents and those who work or wander here an agreeable contrast with the surroundings.

You savor not only the peace but also the restful, harmonious architecture inspired by the neoclassical and neo-renaissance styles. The high point of a stroll is the inner square formed by the compound's dogleg shape, graced by a fountain and trees. All you'd need is a café with sidewalk tables to happily spend a lifetime here.

Musée de la Vie romantique

9TH ARRONDISSEMENT
Entrance: 16, rue Chaptal
Métro: Blanche, Pigalle
Open Tue-Sun 10am-6pm (closed Mon, holidays)

✦

THOUGH IT'S PRIMARILY RESIDENTIAL, THE NINTH ARRONDISSEMENT ISN'T EXACTLY TOP IN ITS CLASS WHEN IT COMES TO PUBLIC PARKS or open spaces. There are only five, with less than one hectare of space all told. Most are near noisy arteries—with the exception of the pocket-sized square Alex-Biscarre near the Saint-Georges métro station. Gardens in this arrondissement are often hidden behind imposing carriage gateways. That's one of many reasons to make a pilgrimage to the Musée de la Vie romantique and its garden—especially its garden.

Everything is wonderful here, starting with the shady lane leading to the garden court where a handful of tables from the museum's tearoom stand, a perfect spot in nice weather for a pick-me-up. Flowers bloom on all sides: old-fashioned roses, campanulas, clematis. The beautiful old trees, greenhouse, rock garden and fountain are also wonderful.

This enchanted spot was the home of painter Ary Scheffer, a member of the Romantic Movement—on the academic side. An illustrative example of his talent is *Les Ombres de Francesca da Rimini et de Paolo Malatesta apparaissent à Dante et à Virgile*, displayed at the Louvre.

Cour intérieure de l'hôpital Saint-Louis

INNER COURTYARD, HÔPITAL SAINT-LOUIS

10TH ARRONDISSEMENT

Entrance: 2, place du Docteur-Alfred-Fournier

Métro: Goncourt, Jacques-Bonsergent

Open weekdays (closed weekends)

✦

SOME MIGHT BE PUT OFF BY THE THOUGHT OF SEEKING A QUIET, LEAFY CORNER IN A HOSPITAL COMPOUND. BUT IT'S PRECISELY IN SUCH ESTablishments that you come across those big signs commanding "Hospital Grounds: Silence!"

Luckily, the main courtyard of the Saint-Louis hospital is remarkable for more than its signage, notably for its landmark value. This is a rare example of gorgeous early-1600s architecture, of the same kind found at the place des Vosges. The two share in common King Henri IV, who commissioned them both to be built, and who gave the go-ahead for the spectacular quadrilateral design combining stonework and brick.

Let not the site's beauty obliterate the memory of the tragic reasons the hospital was created: the horrific plagues of the early 1600s that drove Henri IV to demand the fortress-like structure be set on what was the edge of town, to keep plague victims in and others out. Happily, we walkers of the present day run no risk of being plagued in the tenth arrondissement—at least not by pestilential germs!

Maison de l'architecture

10TH ARRONDISSEMENT

Entrance: 150, rue du Faubourg-Saint-Martin

Métro: Gare-de-l'Est

Open weekdays 10am-6pm, 2-6pm weekends

✦

THIS IS WHERE IN THE EARLY SEVENTEENTH CENTURY, MARIE DE MÉDICIS FOUNDED THE RÉCOLLETS CONVENT, BELONGING TO THE Franciscan order. After being ransacked during the Revolution, it was converted into a barracks, then a wool-spinning works, a hospice for the terminally ill and a military hospital (in 1860). Each remodeling brought changes. Parts were swept away in 1926 when the avenue de Verdun was put through, and again a few years later when the nearby Gare de l'Est was expanded. Declared unsafe, it was closed in 1968; part of its grounds was handed over to the Saint-Louis hospital, and some of the buildings became a school of architecture. Then in 1991, a group of artists squatted the site and were only driven out after a fire. The least that can be said is, the Récollets convent has a checkered past. Today, with the Maison de l'architecture, this historic site has at last found peace. It's officially "a facility with European, even global reach that welcomes artists, researchers, intellectuals and university professors," providing lodging and sometimes workshop space. The public is free to visit, and welcome to attend events, exhibitions and meetings. The lovely garden, in warm weather, is graced by the Café de la Maison.

SCULPTEUR
Tel 0146283894

Cours et passages du Faubourg Saint-Antoine

COURTYARDS AND PASSAGEWAYS OF FAUBOURG SAINT-ANTOINE

11TH AND 12TH ARRONDISSEMENTS
Entrances: rue du Faubourg-Saint-Antoine
Métro: Bastille, Ledru-Rollin
Open daily

✦

PASSAGE DU CHEVAL-BLANC (WHITE HORSE), PASSAGE DE LA BOULE-BLANCHE (WHITE BALL), COUR DU BEL-AIR, PASSAGE DU CHANTIER (builder's yard), cour Saint-Louis, cour du Nom-de-Jésus (the Name of Jesus), cour de l'Étoile d'Or (star of gold), cour des Trois-Frères (three brothers), cour de la Maison-Brûlée (burned house), cour de l'Ours (bear), passage de la Bonne-Graine (good seed), cour du Saint-Esprit, passage de la Main-d'Or (hand of gold). The courtyards and passageways off the rue du Faubourg-Saint-Antoine have catchy names, charged with history, singing with a poetry that the signs of the encroaching, cheap ready-made clothing shops are silting over slowly but surely. Visit before it's too late.

Arboretum de l'École de Breuil, bois de Vincennes

ÉCOLE DE BREUIL ARBORETUM, BOIS DE VINCENNES

12TH ARRONDISSEMENT

Entrances: route de la Ferme, route de la Pyramide

RER: Joinville-le-Pont

Open daily 10am-5pm November-February; 10am-6pm March, October; 10am-7pm April-September. Free weekdays, entrance fee required weekends.

✦

ARE WE REALLY IN PARIS? THE BELTWAY IS FAR BEHIND, AND THE NEAREST TOWN IS ACTUALLY JOINVILLE-LE-PONT. WELL, YES, IN FACT the 995-hectare bois de Vincennes forest is officially part of the city of Paris. Back when it opened in 1936, the école du Breuil—originally the municipal forestry school of suburban Saint-Mandé—was located at porte Dorée on the park's western edge. It moved to the southwest corner of the park some sixty years later. It's worth going out of your way to explore this place. As the name suggests, the arboretum is a veritable museum of the tree—*arbor* in Latin. Here, covering over twelve hectares, about 800 tree species grow. The stars of the show include the caramel tree whose leaves in the fall give off the scent of burnt caramel, or the Cunninghamia tree from China. Rabbits, squirrels, ferrets and hedgehogs happily make their homes in this splendid parkland. We might do worse than join them—or at least pay a visit.

ANGELE
NINOU

Îles du bois de Vincennes

ISLANDS OF THE BOIS DE VINCENNES

12TH ARRONDISSEMENT
Entrance: Lac Daumesnil
Métro: Porte-Dorée
Open daily

✦

SURE, THERE'S THE ÎLE DE LA CITÉ, THE ÎLE SAINT-LOUIS AND EVEN THE ALLÉE DES CYGNES—A NARROW STRIP MIDSTREAM IN THE SEINE between the Bir-Hakeim and Grenelle bridges. But Paris possesses other, lesser-known islands in the lakes of the bois de Boulogne (familiar to readers of Proust's *The Guermantes Way*) and the bois de Vincennes.

The lac Daumesnil in the bois de Vincennes has not one but two islands. The busier of the two is the Île de Reuilly, reached from the mainland on a small bridge. You'll be surprised to discover a faux-Greco-Roman circular temple here, built in the 1860s (it's similar to the one at Buttes-Chaumont), plus an equally faux grotto. From this island you can cross another little bridge to Île de Bercy, which is incredibly peaceful on weekdays. The biggest sycamore in France grows here; it's about 45 meters tall. But the best way of all to enjoy the pleasure of island-isolation is to rent a rowboat and wash up on the deserted shore of your choice.

Jardin et chapelle de la Pitié-Salpêtrière

GARDENS AND CHAPEL, LA PITIÉ-SALPÊTRIÈRE HOSPITAL

13TH ARRONDISSEMENT

Entrance: 47, boulevard de l'Hôpital

Métro: Saint-Marcel, Gare-d'Austerlitz

Open daily 9am-6pm

✦

PARIS' BIGGEST HOSPITAL WAS AN ARMORY UNTIL LOUIS XIV DECIDED TO TURN IT INTO A POORHOUSE. THE ONLY PROPER WAY TO VISIT IS to cross the cour Saint-Louis, a courtyard with a lovely French garden, pause long enough to admire the imposing façade, then step into the chapel for a leisurely perusal. Somber and stern, it sometimes houses temporary exhibitions. Afterwards, enter the cour Mazarin, then follow rue de l'Église—a ticket straight to the countryside. You'll find yourself on the promenade de l'Hauteur, a spacious park dotted with old trees, benches and picnic tables. "No ball-games allowed on the lawns," warns a sign. But who would dream of playing ball here? Lovers prefer to flirt, and nurses to roll *boules* on the gravel lanes.

ST PHILIPPE

SUZE

Buttes aux Cailles

13TH ARRONDISSEMENT

Entrance: rue de la Butte-aux-Cailles and adjoining streets

Métro: Place-d'Italie, Corvisart

Open daily

✦

FAIRLY ANIMATED AT NIGHT BY COPSES OF RESTAURANTS AND BARS (SOME OF THEM PRETTY UNUSUAL), THE BUTTE AUX CAILLES IS perfectly peaceful by day. The neighborhood feel can be downright provincial, and the best way to savor it is to stroll along the hilltop's streets flanked by little low-rise buildings and freestanding houses. Sometimes, as you pass an open gateway, you'll catch a glimpse of a garden, and at many a turn in the slope a novel view will open before your eyes.

Rues pavillonnaires du 13e

BACK STREETS AND GARDEN-HOMES OF THE 13TH

13TH ARRONDISSEMENT

La Petite-Alsace: 10, rue Daviel, Métro: Glacière, Corvisart

Villa Daviel: 7, rue Daviel, Métro: Glacière, Corvisart

Cité Fleurie: 65, boulevard Arago, Métro: Glacière

Villa Auguste-Blanqui: 44, rue Jeanne-d'Arc, Métro: Nationale

Cité Florale: rue Brillat Savarin, rue Auguste-Lançon, Métro: RER Cité-Universitaire

Place de l'Abbé-Georges-Hénocque and surroundings, Métro: Tolbiac

Open daily

✦

THE 13TH ARRONDISSEMENT IS MUCH MORE THAN A CLUTTER OF NEIGHBORHOODS STUDDED WITH HIGH-RISE TOWERS. IT'S ALSO REplete with charming streets, lanes and *cité* or *villa* courtyard-complexes flanked by low, freestanding houses. These are tranquil spots, and often leafy, too, and it's a pleasure to wander through them, gazing with envy at the lucky-few residents. Here's a hit-list that doesn't claim to be exhaustive.

La Petite-Alsace comprises forty brick and half-timbered homes ranged around a sizable courtyard—over 500 square meters—studded with trees. Designed as (and still) a low-income housing project, it was built in 1910 by an Alsatian architect.

Down the road at 7, rue Daviel is the hidden Villa Daviel, a bunch of small working-class houses of yellowish and red bricks, each with a pocket-sized yard.

Cité Fleurie has twenty-nine semi-detached units with exposed timbering, cobbled together in the 1880s from construction material salvaged from the 1878 Universal Exposition, and conceived as workshops-cum-housing. The name is apt: the complex is submerged by vegetation.

Villa Auguste-Blanqui near place Jeanne-d'Arc is composed of twenty tall, narrow houses with tiny courts or gardens.

Cité Florale is actually several streets, each with an evocative, flowery name: rue des Orchidées, des Glycines, des Volubilis, des Liserons, des Iris, not to mention the square des Mimosas. Built in 1928, the streets are flanked by freestanding houses of varying—some might say clashing—architectural styles with compact gardens. An enchanting spot far from the noise of the city.

Lastly, an entire quarter centered around irresistible place de l'Abbé-Georges-Hénocque. Here you'll discover peaceful streets like rue Dieulafoy lined by houses with steep, pitched roofs, or rue Henri-Pape, whose stuccoed homes are decorated with ceramics, flanked by semi-detached cottages with stone facing.

Cité internationale universitaire

14TH ARRONDISSEMENT
Entrance: 19, boulevard Jourdan
RER: Cité-Universitaire
Open daily 7am-10pm

✦

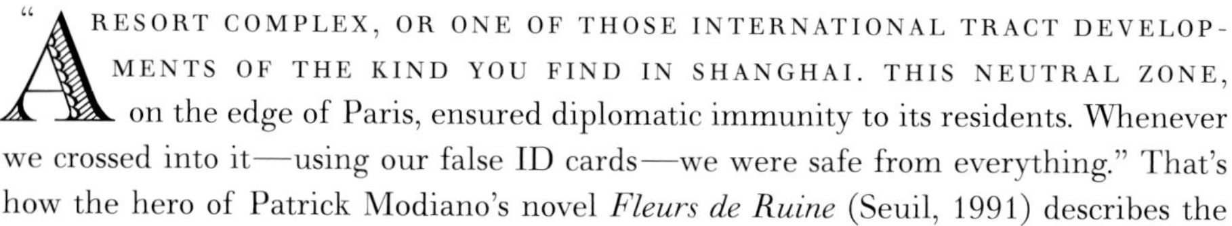

"A RESORT COMPLEX, OR ONE OF THOSE INTERNATIONAL TRACT DEVELOPMENTS OF THE KIND YOU FIND IN SHANGHAI. THIS NEUTRAL ZONE, on the edge of Paris, ensured diplomatic immunity to its residents. Whenever we crossed into it—using our false ID cards—we were safe from everything." That's how the hero of Patrick Modiano's novel *Fleurs de Ruine* (Seuil, 1991) describes the Cité internationale universitaire. How could this complex not have been mentioned in a book largely set in cosmopolitan spots on the edge of Paris?

Mysteriously, the Cité internationale universitaire is often left out when people talk about big open spaces in the capital. But this city-within-the-city is actually a vast park of forty hectares, with 7,000 inhabitants, most of them foreign students from more than 100 countries. Walk through and admire the thirty-seven residential apartment blocks or freestanding houses built in the style of each host country. Then pick a spot and stretch out on the boundless lawn smack in the middle of the campus.

Cloître de Port-Royal, Maternité Baudeloque

PORT-ROYAL CLOISTER, BAUDELOQUE MATERNITY HOSPITAL

14TH ARRONDISSEMENT

Entrance: 123, boulevard de Port-Royal

RER: Port-Royal

Open daily

✦

IN HIS *DICTIONNAIRE ÉROTIQUE* (PAYOT, 1993), PIERRE GUIRAUD IDENTIFIES 530 WORDS AND EXPRESSIONS RELATED TO THE FEMALE SEXUAL organ, among them *cloître* (cloister). Well, why not? After all, a cloister is an enclosed place that not just any Tom, Jack or Harry can enter. And if convents and monasteries have one undeniable virtue, it's the way they've inspired authors of erotic literature.

No licentiousness here, however. This cloister is in a maternity hospital. It started life as the abbey of Port-Royal which, beginning in 1625, housed the Sisters of the Holy Sacrament from the other Port-Royal abbey in suburban Champs. Naturally, like other convents in Paris, Port-Royal has led a checkered life.

Depending on weather and mood, you might want to perch under one of the arcades running along three of the cloister's sides. Or you might prefer one of the four benches in the French garden filling the cloister's center, planted with primly trimmed yews. Stay for as long as you like.

Cité des Arts

14TH ARRONDISSEMENT
Entrance: 21, avenue du Maine
Métro: Montparnasse-Bienvenüe
Open daily

✦

IN THIS ANIMATED NEIGHBORHOOD THAT LIVES IN THE CRUSHING SHADOW OF THE MONTPARNASSE TOWER, IT'S A NICE SURPRISE TO come across this quiet, leafy cul-de-sac. It's hard to imagine, but in the nineteenth century there was a coaching inn here whose stagecoaches served France's western routes. In the 1900s, this garden-court welcomed the *crème* of the modern art world: Picasso, Braque, Modigliani, Léger, Derain, Cendrars, Max Jacob, Cocteau, Foujita, Soutine and many others. That's because in the early years of the century, the owner had thirty artists' studios built on the property using materials salvaged from the Universal Exposition of 1900. Marie Vassilieff was one of the renters, and during the First World War she set up the Cantine des artistes in her studio. Often penniless, artists flocked here for a cheap feed and the free conferences, debates and literary or musical soirées Vassilieff organized. At the end of the road a small museum tells the tale of Montparnasse's glory days.

Parc Montsouris

14TH ARRONDISSEMENT

Entrances: boulevard Jourdan, avenue Reille, rue Gazan, rue de la Cité-Universitaire, rue Hansouty, rue Émile-Deutsch-de-la-Meurthe

Métro: RER Cité-Universitaire

Open weekdays 8am-5:30pm (9am weekends; until 9:30pm in summer)

✦

LIKE HUMANS, PUBLIC PARKS HAVE BODY CLOCKS: SLOW-GOING IN THE MORNING AND SLEEPY IN THE LATE AFTERNOON. AND IT'S PRECISELY in these cottony moments that you should sneak up on them, holding your breath.

The parc Montsouris is no exception to the rule. Inspired by London, the park covers ten hectares of sprawling lawns peppered with century-old trees, plus flower beds and clumps of shrubbery, and the requisite Haussmann-style appurtenances: lakes, waterfalls, bridges, a tunnel, sculpture.

The park's trimmings—meaning the neighborhood flanking it on the west side—are also appealingly full of surprises, a cityscape of garden-squares, courts and cul-de-sacs starting at rue Nansouty and rue Émile-Deutsch-de-la-Meurthe. Nice big bourgeois homes and spacious art studios live happily side by side, wrapped in greenery. Architecture buffs will certainly recognize one building by Le Corbusier and another by Perret.

Villas et jardins secrets du 14e

VILLAS AND SECRET GARDENS OF THE 14TH

14TH ARRONDISSEMENT

Villa Hallé: 36, rue Hallé, Métro: Mouton-Duvernet
Villa Adrienne: 19, avenue du Général-Leclerc, Métro: Mouton-Duvernet
Villas Deshayes, Duthy, Collet and Mallebay: rue Didot, Métro: Plaisance
Villa Seurat: 101, rue de la Tombe-Issoire, Métro: Plaisance
Open daily

✦

HAPPY ARE THOSE ARRONDISSEMENTS THAT HAVE KEPT ALIVE THE MEMORY—RATHER RECENT—OF THE DAYS WHEN YOU COULD still dream of building your own freestanding house in Paris. The thirteenth arrondissement has its charming old low-cost housing projects, but the fourteenth is at once more bourgeois and arty.

In French, villa can mean a mansion or, more commonly, a garden-home complex centered on a narrow street. In the heart of rue Hallé among nicely matched houses and small apartment buildings, the villa Hallé hides its cobbled lane flanked by low-rise homes in a variety of styles, most of them wrapped in pocket-sized gardens that buffer them from view.

Villa Adrienne is one of the stars of the arrondissement. Dating to the late 1800s, its buildings surround

a vast garden. Lawns, towering trees and benches welcome passersby.

Many villas branch off rue Didot on both the odd- and even-numbered sides near the Broussais hospital. Here, too, you'll find a mix of houses, studios and low buildings in a variety of architectural styles—some a tad clunky—cloaked in greenery.

Like its near-contemporary rue Mallet-Stevens (in the sixteenth arrondissement), the villa Seurat was almost entirely the work of a single architect: André Lurçat. In the 1920s, he designed and built beautiful townhouses for his wealthy artist friends, in the modernist style of his day.

Villa Santos-Dumont

15TH ARRONDISSEMENT
Entrance: rue Santos-Dumont
Métro: Convention, Porte-de-Vanves
Open daily

✦

LIVE IN YOUR OWN HOUSE IN PARIS? THAT'S PRETTY MUCH A DREAM. BUT IT'S REALITY FOR THE INHABITANTS OF THE CAPITAL'S 130 ZONES designated by urban planners for individual homes or villas.

Villa Santos-Dumont is a fine specimen in its class, a blend of workshops or studios and stone-faced houses. Singer-songwriter Georges Brassens was a longtime resident. The rue Santos-Dumont is also a charmer, lined by small 1920s tract homes with red-tile roofs and miniature gardens.

Square Blomet

15TH ARRONDISSEMENT
Entrance: 43, rue Blomet
Métro: Volontaires
Open daily 9am-5pm (until 9pm in summer)

✦

IS *PÉTANQUE* THE MOST POPULAR SPORT PLAYED IN PARIS? MAYBE NOT, THOUGH ASTONISHINGLY ENOUGH THERE ARE FIFTY *PÉTANQUE* associations in the capital. Some have their bowling alleys wedged between sidewalks and busy streets, while others boast a nicer setup. Here's one of the winners, in the fifteenth arrondissement, where bowlers are welcome to play in the handsome square Blomet. When the weather's nice, it's great to settle down on a strategically placed bench facing the outdoor bowling alleys. Savor the sublimely relaxing provincial atmosphere with an almost Mediterranean feel… right down to the sweet scent of aniseed-flavored pastis. *So, are you tossing or marking?*

Musée Bourdelle

15TH ARRONDISSEMENT
Entrance: 18, rue Antoine-Bourdelle
Métro: Montparnasse-Bienvenüe, Falguière
Open Tue-Sun 10am-6pm (closed Mon, holidays)

✦

CLOSE YOUR EYES. THE RUMBLE OF MONTPARNASSE—LOOMINGLY CLOSE—SUDDENLY DISAPPEARS. BIRDS CHIRP. GRAVEL CRUNCHES underfoot. It's not the countryside but almost. You're in the garden of the Bourdelle museum, where sculptor Antoine Bourdelle (1861-1929) lived and worked. He himself planted the acacia trees that frame a handful of his bronze sculptures.

The museum was enlarged in 1961 and 1992 to better present more of Bourdelle's often monumental artworks. Our favorite feature here is still the workshop, maintained intact, from the many-paned windows to the worm-eaten furniture, the wobbly staircase to the creaking parquet floor. Close your eyes...

Jardin du Panthéon bouddhique

GARDEN, BUDDHIST PANTHEON

16TH ARRONDISSEMENT
Entrance: 19, avenue d'Iéna
Métro: Iéna
Open Wed-Mon 10am-6pm (closed Tue)

✦

SINCE ITS RECENT RENOVATION, THE MUSÉE GUIMET, WITH ITS COLLECTION OF ASIAN ART, GETS A FAIR SHARE OF ATTENTION, BUT NOT its annex, the Panthéon bouddhique. True, the focus here is narrower: religious artworks brought back from China and Japan by collector Émile Guimet. There's open access—no ticket to buy—so go ahead and enjoy the small back garden.

Inspired by Japan, the enclave was recently restored specifically with Japanese tea gardens in mind. That's why the pavilion was added as a venue for tea ceremonies. This is how its designers describe the ensemble: "The itinerary prepares the heart and soul for the tea ceremony. Plantings include giant bamboo and, together with the water, stones and play of shadow-and-light seek to instill serenity. The garden's treasure-hunt and maze configuration helps visitors feel far from the outside world. The spacing on land or water of the *tobi-ishi* ('flying stone') stepping-stones imposes a rhythm. A wide, zigzag-shaped bridge crosses the ponds: it is an 'intentional fracturing of the space' that 'overturns the relative order of the material elements in situ.' As participants in the tea ceremony approach along the itinerary, they are able to symbolically purify their hands and lips by rinsing them at the basin carved from Brittany granite…" Without doubt, this quiet Japan-imbued corner is among the capital's top Zen spots.

Villa Mulhouse

16TH ARRONDISSEMENT
Entrance: 86, rue Boileau
Métro: Exelmans
Open daily

✦

HAMEAU BOILEAU, VILLA BEAUSÉJOUR, VILLA MONTMORENCY, VILLA DE LA RÉUNION...IT'D BE NICE TO STROLL FREELY THROUGH THESE big old high-class tract developments that feel like villages unto themselves—the hameau Boileau, for instance, with its peaceful streets, squares and garden-home villa complexes composed of many architectural styles (Gothic, 1930s, Norman, Swiss...). But residents see things differently: these places are closed to the public. Fair enough, the people who live here have a right to peace and quiet.

Happily, however, a few similar spots are open to all, including villa Mulhouse, which includes the villas Dietz-Monnin, Émile-Meyer, Cheysson and villa de l'avenue Georges-Risler. The sixty or so cottages arranged around narrow roads and alleys aren't ostentatious, and their gardens are more like small yards. We're a long way from the luxe of the aforementioned enclaves. The fact is, at the end of the nineteenth century this homey quarter was still dotted with factories, and the housing was built for workers. The factories and workers are long gone, but the villa Mulhouse remains, a reminder of a bygone era.

Maison de Balzac

16TH ARRONDISSEMENT
Entrance: 47, rue Raynouard
Métro: Passy, RER: Avenue-du-Président-Kennedy
Open Tue-Sun 10am-6pm (closed Mon, holidays)

✦

PARIS WAS ONE OF BALZAC'S FAVORITE BACKDROPS. THE NOVELIST LIVED IN THE CAPITAL BUT WAS ALWAYS ON THE MOVE, EVADING the repo men that badgered him after several ruinous publishing ventures. Of the eleven places Balzac lodged, this is the only one left, his home for seven happy years. He signed the lease using the name "M. de Breugnol." He adored this address above all because the house was shielded from view by a garden. Another bonus was the secret side door on quiet rue Berton that made it easy to slip out unnoticed.

For his beloved Madame Hanska, from his garden Balzac picked violets "raised in the sunshine of Paris, in the CO_2-charged air that makes flowers and books grow like mushrooms." The pollution problem persists, and the garden is as attractive as ever.

Passage des Eaux

16TH ARRONDISSEMENT

Entrances: 9-13, rue Raynouard, rue des Eaux

Métro: Passy

Wine Museum open Tue-Sun 10am-6pm (closed Mon)

✦

IT WAS WAY BACK IN THE MID-1600S WHEN THIS PASSAGEWAY WAS BEING BUILT—"A STRANGE STAIRCASE STRANGLED BY NEIGHBORING garden-walls," as Zola put it—that a spring with curative powers suddenly welled up unbidden. For decades thereafter, Parisian high society took up residence here, drawn by the famous, reputedly miraculous waters—*les eaux*. A certain abbot named Le Ragois applied himself vigorously as their promoter. The Revolution brought the waterworks to a temporary halt. Later, around 1800, the Delessert family revived the business and even built a thermal health resort here (it was demolished in 1913 to make way for the métro). Only the underground parts of the resort remain and are today home to the Museum of Wine.

Eglise suédoise

THE SWEDISH CHURCH

17TH ARRONDISSEMENT

Entrance: 9, rue Médéric

Métro: Courcelles

Tue-Thur 10am-10pm, Fri and Sun 10am-6pm, Sat noon-6pm

✦

THIS TYPICAL SWEDISH-STYLE BRICK BUILDING AND FORECOURT ARE GUARANTEED TO WHISK YOU AWAY TO THE LAND OF PANCAKES. THE church is under the orders of the archbishop of Stockholm (as are all Swedish Lutheran parishes). Only Swedish is spoken and preached hereabouts. And it's a woman who watches over Paris' Swedish faithful.

The small forecourt of the *svenska kyrkan* is a swell spot for a welcome rest accompanied, perhaps, by a Swedish pastry and a cup of tea. FYI, in Swedish *hej* means "hello," *tack* is "thanks" and *hejdå* is "goodbye."

Be warned, this nifty Swedish enclave gets crowded around Saint Lucy's Day (December 13th) and Christmas, too.

Cité des Fleurs

17TH ARRONDISSEMENT

Entrances: 154, avenue de Clichy; 59, rue de la Jonquière

Métro: Brochant

Open daily

✦

SOMETIMES FOR A FLEETING MOMENT THE IRON GRILLWORK AND GREENERY MAKE THIS SPOT FEEL LIKE IT'S BEEN LIFTED FROM Dinard, in Normandy, near the Atlantic coast. But we're right in the heart of Paris, and the sound of those waves you hear plashing like white music is actually traffic on the avenue de Clichy. Let's not spoil the party. This leafy urban eddy built in the mid-1800s is as pleasant as a bouquet of its poetic namesake *fleurs*.

Butte Montmartre

18TH ARRONDISSEMENT

Allée des Brouillards: rue Girardon, place des Quatre-Frères-Casadesus
Villa Léandre: 23 bis, avenue Junot
Maquis de Montmartre: 65, rue Lepic
Métro: Lamarck-Caulaincourt
Open daily

✦

THE MAGIC OF BIG CITIES IS THAT THEY OFFER INTREPID WALKERS THE CHANCE TO SLIP AWAY FROM THRONGED THOROUGHFARES ONTO byways seemingly unbeaten in recent decades by human feet. Despite being the homeland of Amélie Poulain and Paris' prototypical tourist trap, Montmartre happily conforms to this rule of serendipity.

To the French ear, the first appealing thing about allée des Brouillards is the name—"fog alley." It wells up from the distant seventeenth century, when a small farm and millhouse stood here. Some say the fog arose on stormy days, while others insist that nearby springs disgorged mist, thereby hatching the unusual place-name.

No matter: this narrow lane is magical, in part because of the so-called château des Brouillards, recently restored after decades

of abandonment. Writer Gérard de Nerval lodged here. And Roland Dorgelès titled one of his novels *Château des Brouillards*.

Follow the lovely, mansion-lined avenue Junot to villa Léandre, charming for its own good reasons. Oddly, it seems to whisk visitors to a London cul-de-sac. Might it be the paving, rampant vegetation and British architecture from the 1920s? And what of the silence that fills this atmospheric dead-end street?

The quiet is all the more uncanny a few steps away in *le maquis*. This urban garden is a kind of sublime, glorified warren of vacant lots, the last vestige of the shantytown where a century ago the Butte's penniless daubers, thieves, grifters and drifters sheltered. Most of *le maquis* was transformed years ago into a park. Nowadays you're more likely to run into *pétanque* bowlers lording over it—chic and savvy enough to have appropriated one of the capital's most pleasant hideaways.

Cimetière de Montmartre

MONTMARTRE CEMETERY

18TH ARRONDISSEMENT

Entrance: 20, rue Rachel

Métro: Place-de-Clichy, Blanche

Open daily 8am-5:30pm (from 8:30am Sat; 9am Sun) Nov 6-March 15; until 6pm from March 16-Nov 5

✦

"THE DEAD UNDERGROUND WE LAY, AND THERE THEY STAY." IF THE THOUGHT OF RESTING IN PEACE (TEMPORARILY, OF COURSE) IN A graveyard gives you the creeps, ward off evil spirits by reciting that little ditty from *La Complainte de l'oubli des morts* by Jules Laforgue. Then explore this vast, eleven-hectare compound that's less crowded than celebrated Père-Lachaise cemetery. Hilly, green and very peaceful, this enclave is just two minutes on foot from place de Clichy. Amid the sumptuous tombs set on gravel lanes—no expense was spared on sepulchres in the nineteenth century—you'll run into few tourists, seniors come to polish a tombstone, Dalida fans and the occasional sauntering *flâneur*. The "residents," so to speak, are sure to please all customers. There's Stendhal and François Truffaut, not to mention Théophile Gautier, Gustave Moreau, Offenbach and Sacha Guitry.

Before you leave, have a thought for old Jules Laforgue—he's not buried here, but rather in suburban Bagneux: "The dead/They're discreet/They sleep/Too cool for comfort."

Eglise Saint-Serge

CHURCH OF SAINT-SERGE

19TH ARRONDISSEMENT

Entrance: 93, rue de Crimée

Métro: Laumière, Ourcq

Open daily 6-7pm (10am-12:30pm Sun, during services)

✦

THE FACT THAT THE CHURCH OF SAINT-SERGE IS LISTED IN MANY GUIDEBOOKS COULD LEAD YOU TO FEAR THE WORST—AN INVASION of visitors, signage everywhere, long waiting lines, snack bars and souvenir stands. Happily not. The default setting here is peace, and peaceful the place remains no matter what.

You can't see the church from the street. But step through a gate, follow the driveway and you'll discover this former Lutheran place of worship, transformed into a Russian Orthodox church with two onion domes—one red, the other blue—and a gaily painted wooden staircase. To round things off, there are benches in the yard where you can rest, relax and gather your thoughts.

La Mouzaïa

19TH ARRONDISSEMENT

Entrances: rue de Mouzaïa, rue David-d'Angers,
rue Miguel-Hidalgo, rue du Général-Brunet
Métro: Danube, Pré-Saint-Gervais, Botzaris
Open daily

✦

LA MOUZAÏA IS THE NAME OF A NEIGHBORHOOD THAT HAS PARIS' LARGEST NUMBER OF LOW-RISE, FREESTANDING OR SEMI-DETACHED GARDEN-homes—hundreds of them strung along some thirty streets, villa and hamlet complexes and cul-de-sacs. Why here? Because the quarter sits atop former gypsum quarries, in use until the nineteenth century, then filled and built over. The unstable soil can't bear weighty buildings.

It's lovely to get lost wandering down these streets or narrow alleys, some of them set at a tilt, most garlanded by greenery that often submerges yards and houses. Many are modest, in keeping with their original, largely blue-collar inhabitants. Others stand three or four stories tall; still others are half-timbered. Dreamily strolling from one leafy lane to the next, you'll gradually forget the twenty-first century and the rumbling city out there, and be sorely tempted to ring someone's bell simply to ask if life really is as sweet here as it seems to a passing stroller.

Butte Bergeyre

19TH ARRONDISSEMENT

Entrances: rue Barrelet-De-Ricou, rue Philippe-Hecht, rue Michel-Talgrine

Métro: Bolivar, Buttes-Chaumont, Colonel-Fabien

Open daily

✦

EVERY PARISIAN KNOWS BUTTES-CHAUMONT, BUTTE MONTMARTRE AND BUTTE AUX CAILLES. BUT ONE URBAN MOUNT IS STILL UNSUNG: Butte Bergeyre. Its handful of streets perched at an altitude of 100 meters was built in 1920 in place of a planned stadium. Here's how lucky residents describe their crow's nest on www.habitants.bergeyre.free.fr: "Unstable landfill veined with quarries, low buildings, grapevines, handsome houses, leaky pipes, nice views of Paris and that plaster-cast church atop Montmartre, traffic signs, a bistro… that doesn't exist, ditto the public garden… parked cars, hangouts where locals chat and more if they feel like it, and a few cats lazing in the sun, weather permitting (not an exhaustive list)."

While we're at it, let's add two honorary citizens to this charming village: rue Rémy-de-Gourmont and rue Edgar-Poë, names that make lovers of eighteenth-century literature dream.

Parc des Buttes-Chaumont

BUTTES-CHAUMONT PARK

19TH ARRONDISSEMENT

Entrances: rue Manin, rue Botzaris

Métro: Buttes-Chaumont, Botzaris

Open daily 7am-8:15pm (Sept-May), until 9:15pm in spring, 10:15pm in summer

✦

"DURING THOSE MARVELOUS, SORDID TIMES, I ALMOST INVARIABLY PREFERRED THE TIMES' PREOCCUPATIONS TO MY OWN HEART'S occupations, and lived a chance existence, in pursuit of chance, which alone among the divinities had shown itself capable of retaining its authority."

So begins *A Feeling for Nature at the Buttes-Chaumont*, the second part of Louis Aragon's *Paysan de Paris* (Paris Peasant). It's a strange, sui generis book published in 1926. To be read, perhaps, on a sloping lawn at this, the third-largest Paris public garden after the Tuileries and parc de la Villette—a place where above all you can savor the charming serenity of a Second Empire retreat.

Jardin naturel

NATURAL GARDEN

20TH ARRONDISSEMENT

Entrances: rue de la Réunion, rue de Lesseps

Métro: Alexandre-Dumas

Open daily 9am-5:30pm in winter, until 9pm in summer

✦

A*RTEMISIA ABSINTHIUM*, POPPIES, FERNS, COLUMBINE, PRIMULAS, CLEMATIS, WILD CARROTS AND HYACINTH, BLOOD-WORTS, POTENTILLA. RED dragonflies, frogs, salamanders and newts, water spiders, toads and snails. Crowded together, they live cheek-by-jowl in this organic compound where herbicides, pesticides and watering are strictly forbidden. There's a pond with water lilies and reeds, a mini-prairieland dotted with wildflowers and a thicket of birches and maples. The natural setting is, well...*très naturelle,* and located just beyond the side entrance to Père-Lachaise cemetery.

La Campagne à Paris

THE COUNTRYSIDE IN PARIS

20TH ARRONDISSEMENT

Entrances: rue Irénée-Blanc, rue Jules-Siegfried, rue Paul-Strauss

Métro: Porte-de-Bagnolet

Open daily

✦

THE VERY NAME MAKES YOU DREAM. BUT DON'T EXPECT TO FIND WHEAT FIELDS, COWS AND PATHS TANGLED WITH BRAMBLE AND blackberries. "Campagne à Paris" is actually the name of a low-cost co-op housing association that bought up sizeable land tracts about a century ago, parcels no one wanted—for good reason: they were quarries filled with rubble from the rebuilding of Paris under Baron Haussmann during the Second Empire. The idea was to create housing for low-income families. The First World War slowed the project, inaugurated only in 1926.

Along the three streets that comprise this swath of urban countryside stand about ninety houses built of brick, with stone or stucco facing, each with a tiny forecourt and mini-back yard. Flowers and shrubbery provide the finishing touches.

Lovers of Paris trivia will thrill to discover one of the city's smallest "streets" here, rue Georges-Perec, in reality a mere staircase linking rue Jules-Siegfried and rue Paul-Strauss. Perec, the fanciful author of *Les Choses*, would doubtless be tickled by this non-street with not a single numbered address!

Cimetière de Charonne

CHARONNE CEMETERY

20TH ARRONDISSEMENT

Entrance: 111, rue de Bagnolet

Métro: Porte-de-Bagnolet

Open daily 8am-5:30pm (from 8:30am Sat; 9am Sun) Nov 6-March 15; until 6pm from March 16-Nov 5

✦

A MODEST CHURCH, THE PRIEST'S LITTLE GARDEN, AND RIGHT BEHIND, THE CEMETERY. ONLY IN THE PROVINCES CAN YOU SET SUCH A SCENE. Not really: here you're in a part of the former village of Charonne that was created before Charonne was swallowed by the capital.

Touching in its simplicity, a visit to Saint-Germain-de-Charonne is a must. Churches are among those rare places in Paris where you can be sure to find true silence. Those who go boldly into these sanctuaries also often discover overlooked art and architectural treasures.

Now follow the path alongside the magnificent presbytery garden—where flowers, vegetables and fruit trees grow side by side—toward the tombs. It's a small graveyard without many celebrated residents, except perhaps Robert Brasillach, Gérard Bauër (a talented but now forgotten chronicler), actor Pierre Blanchar or (former culture minister) André Malraux's two sons, who died tragically. Oh, and François Bègue, alias Père Magloire, a house painter who pretended to be Robespierre's secretary.

The church bell is tolling. It's time to cross rue de Bagnolet to rue Saint-Blaise and continue our visit to the former village of Charonne.

FAMILLE AUBRUN

Cimetière du Père-Lachaise

PÈRE-LACHAISE CEMETERY

20TH ARRONDISSEMENT

Entrances: boulevard de Ménilmontant, rue de la Réunion, rue du Repos

Métro: Philippe-Auguste, Père-Lachaise, Gambetta

Open daily 8am-5:30pm (from 8:30am Sat; 9am Sun) Nov 6-March 15; until 6pm from March 16-Nov 5

✦

"I SAW RIGHT AWAY THAT THIS CEMETERY WASN'T LIKE OTHERS, NOT LIKE THE ONE IN OUR VILLAGE, FOR INSTANCE, BEHIND THE TENNIS courts, where an invisible hand throws the ball back each time it goes over the wall. Here you can tell by the tall, halfmoon gateway, the gentle sloping green paradises, the twisting rockery of mausoleums that this cemetery already belongs to the other world. Before you even step inside you sense you will never know it all, you'll never come to the end of its labyrinth of alleyways, or the prayers and wanderings they inspire. That chapel, up there, that you climb terraces to reach, that light blue patch over the chimneys, those fervent poplars, like well-tempered cypresses—it's a heavenly corner in a suburb of petty crime and, in the symphony you leave behind, it's an organ fugue on powerful organs."

—Antoine Blondin, *L'Humeur vagabonde* (La Table Ronde, 1955)

Ilots caches du 20e

HIDDEN ENCLAVES OF THE 20TH

20TH ARRONDISSEMENT

Villa Godin: 85, rue de Bagnolet, Métro: Alexandre-Dumas
Villa and cité de l'Ermitage: 12, rue de l'Ermitage and 315, rue des Pyrénées, Métro: Ménilmontant, Jourdain
Villa du Borrégo: 33, rue du Borrégo, Métro: Saint-Fargeau
Villa Saint-Fargeau: 25, rue Saint-Fargeau, Métro: Saint-Fargeau
Passage des Soupirs: 242, rue des Pyrénées; 47, rue de la Chine, Métro: Gambetta
Open daily

✦

"SOS! ABUSED ARRONDISSEMENT!" THAT'S KIND OF WHAT YOU FEEL LIKE SHOUTING WHEN YOU THINK ABOUT WHAT'S HAPPENED TO THE TWENtieth arrondissement since 1860, when Paris grew from twelve to twenty arrondissements. Belleville, Ménilmontant and Charonne—formerly small villages—

became part of the capital. For each of them the twentieth century proved pitiless, whether the motivations were good or bad. Despite widespread demolitions and the proliferation of housing projects, a number of hidden enclaves have survived. You have to seek them out in this high-contrast arrondissement. Here are a few: villa Godin, villa and cité de l'Ermitage, villas du Borrégo and Saint-Fargeau and passage des Soupirs—the delightful name makes you sigh.

Index

PARKS, GARDENS AND SQUARES

VILLAS, CUL-DE-SACS AND *PLACES*

RUES AND BACKSTREETS

COVERED GALLERIES AND *PASSAGES*

ART GALLERIES

HILLS AND *BUTTES*

CLOISTERS AND COURTYARDS

ABOUT THE AUTHOR

Jean-Christophe Napias lives in Paris. Author, editor, journalist and translator, he has created with his wife a series of guides to Paris, *Paris est à nous*, which has more than seventy titles. He lives in the hip and lively Bastille neighborhood, and dreams of one day moving to a house with a large garden. Until then, he looks for tranquility and nature wherever he can.

ABOUT THE PHOTOGRAPHER

Christophe Lefébure, a graduate of the Institut d'Etudes Politiques de paris with a master's degree in history, combines the qualities of a writer with those of a photographer. His principal subject of study is rural life, its customs and traditions. For several years now, he has expanded his research to Paris. His first work, *La France des lavoirs*, received the Grand Prix Littéraire du Tourisme.

ABOUT THE TRANSLATOR

David Downie is the author of *Cooking the Roman Way*, *Irreverent Guide to Amsterdam* and *Enchanted Liguria*. His travel, food and arts features have appeared in more than fifty magazines and newspapers worldwide, including *Gourmet*, *Bon Appetit*, *Gastronomica*, the *Los Angeles Times Magazine* and *Town & Country Travel.*